A CHILD'S TREASURY of BIBLE STORIES

STAMPLEY

© Creation, text and illustrations: A.M. Lefevre, M. Loiseaux, M. Nathan–Deiller, A. Van Gool
Published and produced by C4Ci, Belgium
This edition has been published for
C.D. Stampley Enterprises, Inc., Charlotte, NC, USA. Email: info@stampley.com
ISBN 1–58087–072–4 Stampley code 0375
Printed in Dubai, (U.A.E.)– 2003

www.stampley.com

CONTENTS

THE OLD TESTAMENT

THE NEW TESTAMENT

THE CREATION OF THE WORLD

In the beginning, God created the heavens and the earth. All was dark, and deep water covered the land. God's Spirit hovered over the water. Then God said, "Let there be Light!"

At once bright rays of light shone down gently on the earth. God saw that this was good, and God separated the light from the darkness. He called the light 'day', and the darkness 'night'. This was the first day.

Then God said, "Let there be a sky to separate the waters, so that water is above the sky and below the sky." And it was so. Night fell, and a new morning dawned. This was the second day.

(Genesis 1:1–8)

On the third day God said, "Let the waters below the sky gather together and let dry ground appear."

God called this dry ground 'land' and the waters 'sea'. And at God's command grass and plants grew across the earth. Flowers blossomed and trees bearing rich fruit burst toward the sky.

On the fourth day God placed the sun in the sky to bring warmth and light to the earth. Night fell and God created the stars and the moon to fill the darkness above the earth.

On the fifth day God said, "All kinds of fish shall fill the oceans, and birds shall fill the sky." And so the birds and the fish were the first creatures to live on the earth.

(Genesis 1:9–23)

On the sixth day God said, "Now the earth shall be filled with life." From the greatest animal to the smallest insect, God made each creature and sent them to live in all four corners of the earth. "Now I will create a being in my own image," He said.

Then God created man in His image. He created both male and female. "You have power over all living things in the sky, on the earth, and in the sea," God told them.

God stopped and looked at all He had created. He said it was very good.

On the seventh day God finished His work. He made this day holy, for this was the day He rested from His work.

(Genesis 1:24–31; 2:1–3)

Adam and Eve

God had planted on earth a beautiful garden, a place called Eden. He had created the garden for Adam, and here He placed the most wonderful plants and creatures.

Looking at the man He had created, God thought, "It is not right that Adam should be alone." So while Adam slept, God took one of his ribs. From this rib He made the first woman, Eve.

God set Adam and Eve in the garden and said: "Everything in this garden is yours. Enjoy it and be happy. Only one thing is forbidden to you. The tree of the knowledge of good and evil grows in this garden. You must never eat any of the fruit from this tree. If you do, you will die."

Adam and Eve were naked, but they were not ashamed, for this is how God had created them.

(Genesis 2:4–25)

Of all the animals that lived in the garden of Eden, the serpent was the most crafty.

"Wouldn't you like to know the secret of this fruit?" he whispered to Eve. "It will give you the knowledge of good and evil, which only God knows. That is why He does not want you to eat it, for then you could be as powerful as He!"

Adam and Eve knew that God had forbidden them to eat the fruit. But Eve thought about the wisdom that could be theirs if they ate the fruit, and she was tempted.

Finally Eve picked one of the forbidden fruits and tasted it. Then she took some to Adam, who also ate the forbidden fruit.

(Genesis 3:1–6)

14

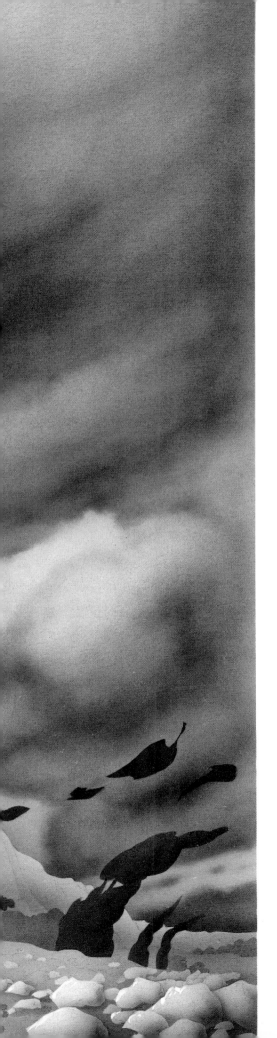

At once their eyes were opened. They saw that they were naked, and for the first time they felt ashamed. They sewed fig leaves together to hide their bodies. When God saw them, He was angry. "Who taught you that you were naked?" He demanded.

"Eve gave me the fruit!" said Adam, and Eve cried, "The serpent tricked me!"

God placed a curse on the serpent. "From now on you will crawl on the ground," He said. Then God turned to Adam and Eve. "From now on your life will be full of suffering," He said. "You have disobeyed me, and from this moment the garden of Eden is forbidden to you."

God drove Adam and Eve out of the garden. God placed an angel with a flaming sword at the entrance to the garden to stop them from ever returning.

(Genesis 3:7–24)

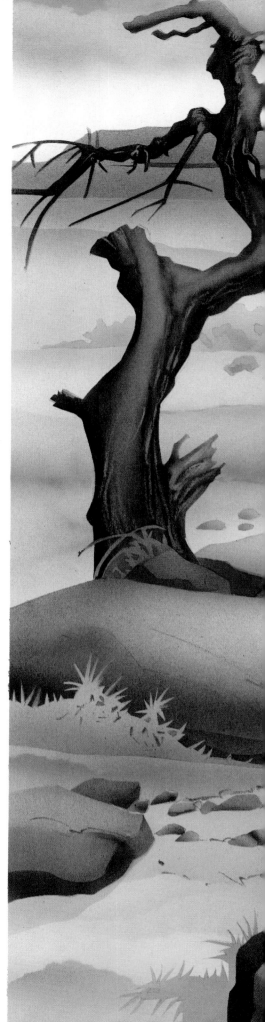

CAIN AND ABEL

After they left the garden of Eden, Adam and Eve had to work very hard. After some time had passed they had two sons, Cain and Abel. The eldest, Cain, farmed and grew crops for food, while Abel tended sheep.

After a time Cain became jealous of his brother. "God must love him more than me," he thought to himself. One day Cain's jealousy got the better of him, and he attacked and killed Abel.

When God asked him where Abel was, Cain answered, "I am not my brother's keeper!" But God knew very well what Cain had done. To punish Cain, God sentenced him to wander the earth, as a fugitive and vagabond. However, God did not want Cain to be killed, so He placed a special mark upon Cain to protect him.

(Genesis 4:1–16)

Noah's Ark

As the years passed, God watched as mankind became more idle and more wicked. The only good people in all the world were Noah and his family, who tried to do what God wanted them to do. "I am going to destroy every living thing on earth," God told Noah. "For mankind must be punished for its wickedness."

God told Noah that He was going to send a huge flood to cover the earth, but that Noah and his family would be spared. "You must build an ark, and into this ark you must lead pairs of every creature. When the flood comes, these will be the only creatures to survive."

Bravely Noah and his family set to work to build the ark as God had commanded. Every day they cut and sawed and hammered. Finally the ark was finished and Noah waited for God to tell him what to do.

(Genesis 6:5–22; 7:1–9)

God then instructed Noah to take his family and his animals into the ark. As soon as the last animals had boarded, the huge door closed. At once heavy rain poured down. The the seas and rivers overflowed, lifting the ark above the ground.

The flood continued for forty days and forty nights, until the earth was completely covered with water. Every living thing on the earth drowned as God had intended. Only Noah and his family and the animals on the ark survived. At last the rain stopped.

For many months, the floodwaters slowly went down. And then one day the ark ran aground and lurched to a halt.

The ark rested on a mountain. Noah sent out a raven to find dry land. The raven never came back. Noah then sent out a dove. But the dove could not find dry land and returned to the ark.

(Genesis 7:10–24; 8:1–9)

A few days later Noah again sent forth the dove. This time the dove found dry land, returning with a tiny olive branch in its beak. "We are saved!" cried Noah.

He waited seven days, then released the dove. It did not return, and Noah realized that the dove had found a place to rest. The waters dropped still further, and at last Noah opened the door. Noah, his family, and all the animals went out of the ark. The hills were beautiful and green. The sky was a bright, clear blue.

Then God promised Noah, "Never again will I destroy the earth with a flood. And every time rainclouds appear over the earth, I will place a rainbow in the sky. This will serve as a sign to remind all creatures of My promise."

(Genesis 8:10–19; 9:8–17)

ABRAHAM

Abraham was descended from Shem, Noah's eldest son. He lived with his wife Sarah in a village near Babel. One day God spoke to Abraham.

"Abraham," He said, "you must leave your home and go on a long journey. Gather all the food and supplies you can carry, and take your wife and servants with you. I am going to lead you to the country that I have chosen for you."

Abraham obeyed at once, and led his household across Mesopotamia and through Egypt. Every night they slept under the stars.
At last they reached the land of Canaan.

(Genesis 12:1–5)

In Canaan, God spoke again to Abraham. "You will live here, and your children and grandchildren after you."

"How is this possible, Lord?" asked Abraham in surprise. "Sarah and I are very old, and we have no children!"

"Abraham," said God, "Do you doubt My word?" Soon afterwards Abraham and Sarah had a son. They named him Isaac.

Some time later God tested Abraham. God told Abraham that he must offer his son as a sacrifice. Abraham loved Isaac. It was with great sadness that he prepared to obey God's command.

Abraham built an altar and laid Isaac upon it. He was lifting his knife to sacrifice the boy, when God spoke again. "Let him go! If you are prepared to give Me your only son, I see how much you must love Me. You are truly blessed among men."

(Genesis 17:1–8; 21:1–3; 22:1–19)

JOSEPH AND HIS BROTHERS

Isaac's son, Jacob, had twelve sons of his own. Joseph, the youngest, was his father's favorite. When Joseph was seventeen, Jacob gave him a wonderful coat. Joseph's brothers were jealous for this coat was more beautiful than anything Jacob had ever given to them. While working in the fields one day, the brothers seized Joseph and tore off his coat.

They were about to kill Joseph but the oldest brother, Reuben, persuaded the others to spare his life. At that moment some merchants came by on their way to Egypt. "This young man will make a good servant!" the brothers cried to the merchants. "Will you buy him from us?" The merchants agreed and took Joseph with them to Egypt.

Joseph's brothers soaked his coat in goat's blood and took it to their father. "Something terrible has happened!" they cried. "Joseph has been killed by a wild beast!"

(Genesis 37:2–33)

While he was a slave in Egypt, Joseph became famous for telling people the meaning of their dreams. Even Pharaoh, the ruler of Egypt, came to see Joseph about a terrible nightmare. Pharaoh told Joseph, "Last night I dreamed of seven fat cows grazing on the banks of the Nile. Suddenly seven thin cows attacked and ate them."

Joseph explained to Pharaoh that God had sent the dream as a warning. Joseph said, "The healthy cows mean that for the next seven years the harvests will be good, and there will be plenty of food. But for seven years after that, the harvests will be poor, and people will starve. This is a warning that you should save grain and corn to see you through the bad years."

Pharaoh was very grateful. As a reward he put Joseph in charge of storing the crops. Joseph became a powerful official in Pharaoh's court.

(Genesis 41:15–40)

MOSES

Jacob's descendants were called Israelites and Hebrews. Many of them lived in Egypt, and the new Pharaoh worried that they were becoming too powerful. "From now on, whenever a baby boy is born to the Hebrews, he must be killed," ordered Pharaoh cruelly.

Moses was born at this time, and his mother was afraid for his life. She wove a basket from rushes and carried it down to the river. Gently laying Moses inside, she placed the basket in the water among some rocks. His sister watched to see what would happen.

Pharaoh's daughter found the basket among the reeds. She was as kind and gentle as her father was cruel. "This must be a Hebrew child," she said to herself. "His parents must want very much to save him." Pharaoh's daughter reared Moses as her own son.

(Exodus 1:6–22; 2:1–10)

As Moses grew up, he saw that the Israelites were treated very badly. One day he saw a soldier beating one of his people. Moses was so angry that he hit the soldier as hard as he could, and the man died. After killing the soldier Moses realized that he must leave Egypt. Moses fled to Midian, where he became a shepherd.

One day Moses was out with his flock when a bush suddenly burst into flames. The flames burned brightly, but to his surprise the leaves and branches of the bush stayed green and fresh.

A voice spoke to him from the bush. "Moses, listen to Me, for this is your God. Your people are suffering under Pharaoh, and you must lead them out of Egypt."

Moses was amazed. "But, Lord," he cried, "no one will listen to a poor shepherd like me!" "Have faith," replied God. "Now go to Pharaoh."

(Exodus 2:11–15; 3:1–12)

As God had commanded, Moses first asked Pharaoh to let the Israelites leave Egypt to go and worship God in the desert. But Pharaoh refused, so God sent a series of plagues to punish him.

First the Nile River and all the water in Egypt turned to blood. Then the land was overrun with frogs. Then everything was infested with gnats, and flies filled the air. The animals died, except those owned by the Israelites, and all the Egyptians suffered painful sores and boils. A great hailstorm destroyed all the crops, and any plants still alive were eaten by a huge swarm of locusts. God plunged the whole land into darkness, but still Pharaoh refused to let the Israelites go.

Finally God sent the most terrible plague of all. His angel visited every household and killed every firstborn male. But God had warned Moses that the angel would pass over the houses of Israelite families who had marked their doorposts with the blood of a lamb sacrificed to God. The Israelite families were not harmed. At last Pharaoh agreed to let Moses lead them out of Egypt.

(Exodus 7–12)

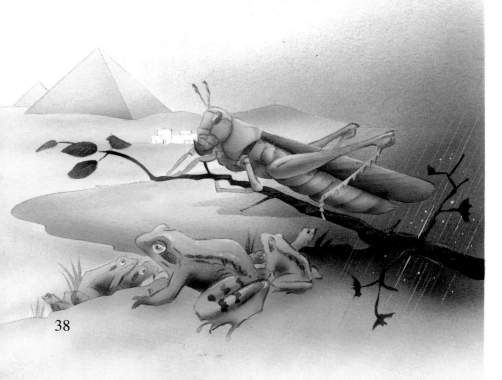

38

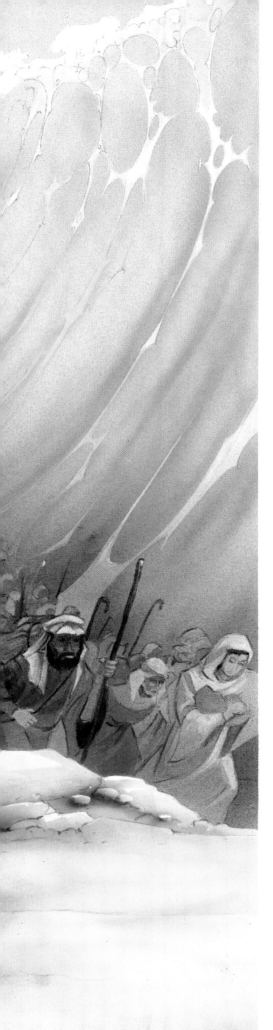

Pharaoh soon regretted his decision to let the Israelites go. He sent a huge army to bring Moses and his people back to Egypt. When the Israelites saw the vast army following them across the desert, they were afraid. "We should never have listened to you!" they complained to Moses. "We would rather be slaves in Egypt than die in the desert!"

"You must have faith," replied Moses. "The Lord will help us." When they reached the Red Sea, the Israelites thought they were truly lost, for there was no way to go forward and escape Pharaoh' soldiers. Then, to their astonishment, the sea parted, leaving a clear path through the waves. "Thank the Lord!" cried Moses, "He has saved us!" Moses led the Israelites safely through the sea.

When Pharaoh's soldiers tried to follow, great walls of water crashed down upon the army and swept it away.

(Exodus 14:5–31)

The Israelites reached Mount Sinai as God had promised. God spoke to Moses once more.

"Moses, these are My commandments, which My people must obey. You shall have no other gods but Me. You shall not make and worship idols. You shall not speak My name with disrespect. The seventh day of the week shall be holy to you, and you shall not work on this day. You shall respect your parents. You shall not murder. You shall not commit adultery. You shall not steal or tell lies against your neighbor, nor must you envy what your neighbor possesses."

Moses came back down the mountain after forty days, carrying the Ten Commandments engraved on two tablets of stone. He found the Israelites worshipping a golden calf. Moses was very angry and ordered the statue destroyed.

(Exodus 19:20–21, 20:1–17, 32:1–20)

42

THE WALLS OF JERICHO

The tablets on which the Ten Commandments were written were kept in a beautiful wooden chest, specially built for the purpose. The chest was known as the Ark of the Covenant.

The Israelites continued their journey in the desert for many years. When they were almost to Canaan, the Promised Land, Moses called Joshua to him. "I am getting old," said Moses. "Soon I will go to God. Be strong and bold, Joshua, for you will lead our people to the Promised Land."

So Joshua led the Israelites into Canaan. They came to the city of Jericho. The city gates were closed. The people would not let the Israelites in.

"Carry the Ark of the Covenant around the city walls seven times," cried Joshua. As they walked, the priests sounded their trumpets. Then the people shouted, and the walls of Jericho came tumbling down.

(Exodus 24–40; Deuteronomy 31:1–8; Joshua 5–6)

SAMSON & DELILAH

The Philistines were angry that the Israelites had returned to Canaan. They declared war on the Israelites, and many battles were fought. Samson, the leader of the Israelite army, loved Delilah, a Philistine woman. Samson was immensely strong, and one night Delilah asked him where his great strength came from. "It comes from God," he replied. "But if my hair were to be cut, I would become weak."

Delilah waited until Samson was asleep, then cut off his long hair. Then she sent for the soldiers who arrested Samson. He was too weak to fight them, and they blinded him and took him to their temple. "Oh Lord, show me favor once more," prayed Samson. He stood between two huge pillars of the Philistine temple and began to push. God had not deserted Samson. The pillars buckled and the temple fell down upon the Philistines.

(Judges 16:4–30)

RUTH AND NAOMI

Since Samson's time, Canaan had become dry and arid, and there was a great famine in the land. Some of the Israelites left and journeyed south. One couple, Elimelech and Naomi, went to live in the neighboring country of Moab. They had two sons, and when these sons grew up they married local women. After many years Elimelech died, and shortly afterwards his two sons fell ill. They also died, leaving Naomi and her daughters -in- law with no one to help them farm the land.

Naomi told her daughters-in-law that she was going to return to Bethlehem. "It is where I was born, and I belong there. You should go back to your parents. I am sure you shall marry again." Orpah, the elder of the two women, said her sad good-byes and left.

But Ruth, the youngest, would not let Naomi travel on her own. "Where you go, I go!" she told Naomi firmly. The two women traveled back to Naomi's hometown of Bethlehem.

(Ruth 1:1–18)

When they reached Bethlehem, Ruth promised
Naomi that she would provide for them both.
Each day she went out into the fields where the
farmers were harvesting their crops and gathered
up the wheat they had dropped.

Boaz, a rich relative of Naomi's, lived in
Bethlehem. He had heard how Ruth looked after
the old woman. One day he stopped Ruth in the
fields. "Everyone is talking of your kindness. You
are a stranger here and your family is far away, yet
you stay to take care of Naomi. You have a soul as
beautiful as your face." He told her that she was
welcome to collect wheat in his fields whenever she
wanted, and Ruth was very grateful.

To Naomi's delight, Boaz and Ruth grew to love
one another and were married.

(Ruth 1:19–22; 2–4)

50

SAMUEL

For many years the prophet Samuel guided the Israelites according to God's word. However, as Samuel grew older, the Israelites decided that they needed a king to rule them. God was displeased that they were turning from Him, and told Samuel to give them a warning. "A king will make slaves of you and your children," said Samuel. "One day you will beg the Lord to save you from your king, but He will not heed you."

The Israelites refused to listen, and chose Saul to be their king. At first Saul was a wise ruler, and God helped him win battles against the Philistines. But he grew proud and arrogant, and began to forget God's commandments.

God told Samuel to travel to Bethlehem. Here lived Jesse, the grandson of Ruth and Boaz. God had chosen David, Jesse's youngest son, to be the new king.

(1 Samuel 8:10; 15–16)

53

DAVID

Meanwhile, Saul's army was about to face the Philistines in another battle. The greatest soldier among the Philistines was called Goliath. Goliath was taller and stronger than any other man. "Saul!" he cried out. "Let us decide the battle by single combat. Will any one of your men dare to fight me alone?" Goliath was so huge that none of Saul's men had the courage to face him.

Suddenly David stepped forward. "I will fight the Philistine," he said. "God is on our side."

Everyone was shocked, for David was just a young boy. He went forward to meet the giant wearing no armor, and carrying only his sling. "Here I am, Goliath," he cried. "I am going to strike you down in God's name!"

Goliath was full of scorn for Saul's champion, and reached for his spear. But David quickly took up his sling and with a single stone he felled the mighty giant.

(1 Samuel 17:1–58)

54

David became so popular that Saul began to hate him. He told his son Jonathan, "Once I am dead, the people may try to make him king instead of you. Something must be done." But Jonathan loved David like a brother, and warned him of the danger. "I know that you will be king in my place, for God has chosen you," he said. "But my father will try to kill you. You must hide." David went into hiding and traveled from place to place.

When Saul learned of David's escape, he set after him at the head of a great army. One night, David crept into the king's camp and stole his spear and water jug. Saul realized how easily David could have killed him, and was ashamed.

Saul finally accepted that David would succeed him, and after Saul's death David was king for forty years. He ruled from Jerusalem and God was with him. Since that time Jerusalem has been known as David's City.

(1 Samuel 18:1–30; 19:1–7; 24–:26; 2 Samuel 5:1–10)

SOLOMON

David's son Solomon succeeded him as king. While Solomon was still a young man, two women came before him. "Sire," said one, "both our babies were born in the same house on the same day. Last night this woman's baby died. She stole my baby while I slept, and says that my child died."

"I did nothing of the sort!" cried the other woman. "It was her baby who died!" Solomon thought for a moment. "There is only one solution to this problem," he said. "I shall cut the baby in two, and each of you shall have half."

One of the women nodded in agreement. The other cried out in horror. "No, don't kill the child!" she sobbed. "Let her keep the baby."

Solomon gave the child to the second woman. "A true mother would rather give up her child than see it killed. The baby is yours." Solomon was known throughout Israel for his wise judgment.

(1 Kings 1:28–30; 2:9–12; 3:16–28)

Unlike other rulers, Solomon befriended the kings of neighboring countries, and there were no wars throughout his long reign. News of his wisdom spread far and wide.

The land was so peaceful, and the people so content that Solomon decided they should build a great temple to God to show Him their thanks.

The temple was built from limestone, and precious woods and metals were brought from afar. When the magnificent temple was completed, Solomon had the Ark of the Covenant carried inside. God told Solomon, "If you or your sons turn away from Me and disobey My laws, I will destroy this temple."

Solomon ruled for forty years, and after his death the peace did not last. There were many wars, and God eventually allowed Jerusalem and the great temple to be destroyed. This was a warning to the Israelites that they had once again forgotten God's commandments.

(1 Kings 4:20–34; 5–8; 11:41–43; 2 Kings 24:20; 25:1–9)

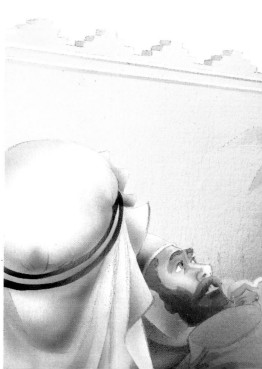

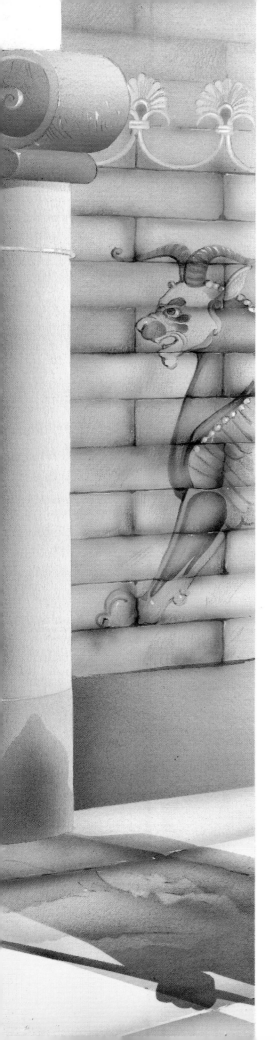

ESTHER

After the destruction of Jerusalem, many Israelites fled to other countries. One man, Mordecai, travelled to Persia. Here he found work at the king's palace in Susa.

Unfortunately he soon became an enemy of Haman, the king's chief minister. Haman was arrogant, and insisted that the workers bow down before him when he passed. Mordecai refused to do this, so Haman hated him. To get his revenge, Haman tried to turn the king against the Israelites. "There are too many of these people in your kingdom, your majesty," he told him. "I fear they may be dangerous."

With the king's authority, Haman planned to kill the Israelites. However, Haman did not know that Esther, the king's favorite wife, was herself an Israelite and neither he nor the king knew that Esther was Mordecai's niece.

(Esther 2:5–7; 17–18; 3:2–14)

Meanwhile, in the palace, Mordecai overheard two men whispering together. To his horror he realized that they were plotting to kill the king!

He hurried to tell Esther, who warned her husband of the plot. The two men were thrown into jail, and the king asked Haman how he should thank the man who had saved his life.

"It is written that the whole city should honor such a man," replied Haman. "Then you must arrange a great feast," commanded the king. The man's name is Mordecai."

Haman was horrified when he learned the hero's name. He had already ordered Mordecai's arrest and execution!

At the feast, Esther explained to the king that the man who had saved his life was an Israelite. "His people are those Haman wants to destroy," she said "and they are my people too!" The king was furious with Haman, and ordered him to be executed in Mordecai's place. Then he made Mordecai his minister.

(Esther 2:19–23; 6:1–14; 7:1–10)

64

DANIEL

In the kingdom of Babylon there lived a young Israelite called Daniel. God had given to Daniel the gift of great wisdom. When the king of Babylon had strange dreams, only Daniel could explain their meaning. However, the king, Nebuchadnezzar, began to believe himself to be even more powerful than God.

Nebuchadnezzar gave the order that all his subjects must worship him as a god, or else be put to death. But Daniel continued to worship the true God. Although he was fond of Daniel, Nebuchadnezzar had him thrown into a den of lions. "Let your God save you!" he said sadly.

The next morning he went to the lion's den, expecting to find Daniel dead. To his surprise the lions were sleeping peacefully at Daniel's feet! "This is truly a miracle!" cried Nebuchadnezzar. "I see now that there is only one true God."

(Daniel 1:17–21; 2:1–45; 3:1–8; 4:1–27; 5:1–31; 6:7–28)

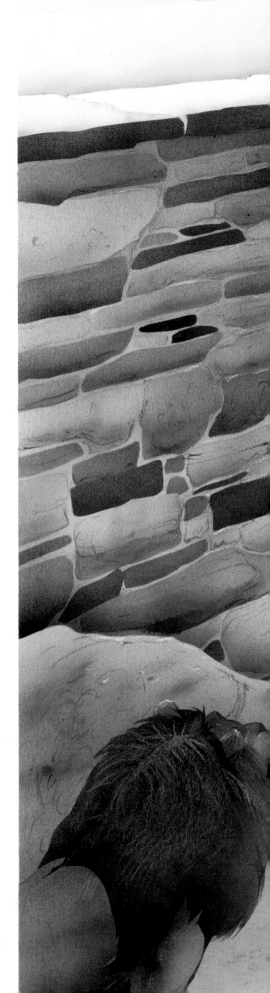

JONAH

In Canaan God spoke to a man named Jonah. "The people in Nineveh are disobeying My word," He said. He asked Jonah to go to Nineveh, in Assyria, and preach there. But Jonah was did not want to go. "I don't like the people of Nineveh. I do not want God to forgive them," he complained.

He tried to hide from God, and traveled to the coast to catch a boat. Hardly had the boat left the shore when it was caught in a terrible storm. "God must be punishing me!" thought Jonah. At once he turned to the sailors and told them to cast him into the sea. "It is the only way you will be saved," he cried. As soon as Jonah plunged into the water, the wind dropped and the sea calmed. But at that moment an enormous fish rose up from the water and swallowed him!

For three days and three nights Jonah remained in the belly of the fish. Then the fish came to the shore and spit him out onto the sand. Once again God told Jonah to go to Nineveh and preach there.

(Jonah 1:1–17; 2:1–10)

Jonah traveled to Nineveh and began to preach God's word, that the city should be destroyed for its sins. But the people of Nineveh listened to Jonah and soon the whole town was living according to God's commandments.

When God forgave the people of Nineveh and did not destroy them, Jonah began once more to complain. "God loves these sinners too well," he thought. "They do not deserve His goodness."

Jonah was so angry he left the town and went into the desert. While Jonah slept, God made a tree grow beside him. Its shade protected him from the hot sun. Then God made the tree wither and die, leaving Jonah at the mercy of the sun's burning rays.

The sun beat upon Jonah's head and he was faint. He asked that he might die. He was angry that the shade plant had withered. God admonished Jonah, "You pity the plant . . . should I not pity Nineveh with its thousands of innocent people. Is a great city not more worthy than a tree"?

(Jonah 3:10; 4:1–11)

AN ANGEL VISITS MARY

During King Herod's reign, a young woman lived in Galilee, in the town of Nazareth. Her name was Mary and she was betrothed to a carpenter called Joseph. One morning an angel appeared to Mary. "Do not be afraid, Mary," he said. "The Lord has sent me with a message for you. He has chosen to honor you above all women. Soon you will bear a son, whom you will name Jesus. He will be called the Son of the Most High, and his kingdom shall last forever."

"How can this be?" asked Mary in wonder, "since I am a virgin?" And the angel told her, "The power of the Holy Spirit shall come upon you, and you shall bear the Son of God."

Mary bowed her head. "I am the servant of the Lord," she replied. "It shall be as you have said."

(Luke 1:26–38)

THE BIRTH OF JESUS

The Israelites who had settled in Judea and Galilee were now known as the Jews, and Herod was their king. But the most powerful ruler in all the land was Augustus, the Roman Emperor.

Some months after Joseph and Mary were married, Augustus wanted to know how many of his subjects lived in each country. He ordered that each person must return to the town of their birth, to sign a register. Joseph and Mary traveled to Bethlehem, where Joseph had been born.

But when they arrived, the inns were full, and they had to stay in a stable. Here Jesus was born.

That night an angel appeared to a group of shepherds watching their flocks in the fields. "I bring you joyful news. Christ the Lord has been born to save mankind. You will find him in a stable, lying in a manger. Go now to Bethlehem and honor him."

(Luke 2:1–20)

THE VISIT OF THE WISE MEN

Far away in the East, wise men had seen a new star in the heavens. They followed the star to Jerusalem and came before King Herod. "We seek the child who has been born King of the Jews," they told Herod. "We have come to worship him." It had been foretold that the King of the Jews would be born in Bethlehem. Herod asked the wise men to send word when they had found the child. "For I wish to honor him myself," he said.

When the wise men found Jesus lying in the stable, they bowed before him and worshiped him. They had brought him precious gifts of gold, frankincense and myrrh.

That night an angel came in a dream and warned the wise men not to return to King Herod. So they went back to their country without traveling through Jerusalem.

(Matthew 2:1–12)

Herod had lied to the wise men. He did not want to worship Jesus. He wanted to kill him. "The people will make him their king, and he will be more powerful than I!" he said.

When he realized that the wise men were not going to return, Herod was furious. He ordered his soldiers to go to Bethlehem and kill every male child under two years of age. But the angel of the Lord appeared to Joseph in a dream and warned him. "Your child is in danger. You must take shelter in Egypt." Joseph took his family and left Bethlehem that same night, and they made the journey into Egypt.

After some years in exile they learned that Herod was dead. Joseph, Mary, and Jesus returned to Israel, to the town of Nazareth.

(Matthew 2:13–22)

JESUS IN THE TEMPLE

Every year, Joseph and Mary went to Jerusalem to celebrate the feast of the Passover. When the festival was finished, they would travel home with a large group of friends and family.

One year, when Jesus was twelve years old, his parents suddenly realized that he was not with them. Joseph and Mary hurried back to Jerusalem. Frightened for his safety, they searched for Jesus for three days. Finally they found him in the temple, where he was talking with the priests and teachers. He amazed everyone with his knowledge and wisdom.

"We were so worried about you, my son," cried Mary. But Jesus replied, "You need not have searched for me. Where else would I be but in my Father's house?"

(Luke 2:41–52)

81

THE BAPTISM OF JESUS

Mary's relative, Elizabeth, also had a son. His name was John and he lived as a hermit on the banks of the Jordan River. People came from all over Judea to hear him preach and to repent of their sins. After they had repented, he baptized them in the river. He became known as John the Baptist.

John told his followers about the prophet Isaiah, who many years before had foretold that a savior would be sent to them. Some people thought that John was the savior. But he told them, "I baptize you with water, but one greater than I will baptize you with the Holy Spirit."

When Jesus was a young man, he went to John, who baptized him in the river. As Jesus stepped out of the water, the Holy Spirit came down upon him. The voice of God spoke from heaven, "This is My Son, whom I love." Then Jesus spent forty days and forty nights in the desert praying to God.

(Matthew 3:1–17; Mark 1:1–11; Luke 1:57–66; John 1:19–34)

THE TWELVE APOSTLES

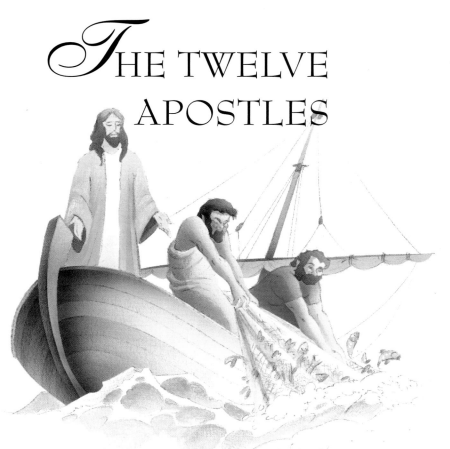

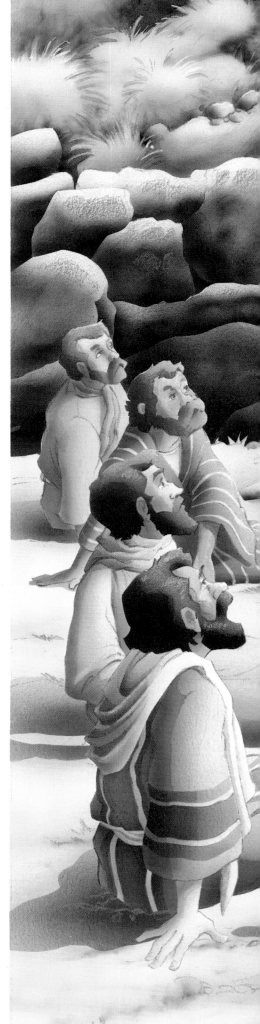

Jesus traveled to Galilee to spread God's word. In every town he visited, crowds gathered to hear him preach. "The Kingdom of God is near," he told them. "It is time to repent of your sins." One day, Jesus passed two fishermen casting their nets into the sea. They were Simon and his brother Andrew. "Leave your nets and follow me," Jesus told them. "I will make you fishers of men."

Simon and Andrew did as Jesus asked, and became his first disciples. More disciples joined him as he traveled, and one day Jesus gathered them around him. From them he picked twelve to be his apostles.

These twelve were Simon (known as Peter), his brother Andrew, James son of Zebedee, his brother John, Philip, Bartholomew, Matthew, Thomas, James, Thaddeus, Simon and Judas Iscariot.

(Matthew 4:17–22; 10:1–4; Mark 1:14–20; Luke 5:–11, 6:12–16)

THE WEDDING AT CANA

In the town of Cana, Jesus was invited to a wedding. The apostles were with him, and so was Mary, his mother.

After some time, Mary saw that all the wine had been consumed. She told Jesus, and Jesus told the servants to fill six large jars with water. "Now fill a cup and take it to the host." The servants did as he told them.

When the host drank from the cup, he turned to the bridegroom. "This wine is excellent. Most people serve the best wine first and save the cheaper wine until the guests have drunk too much. But you have served your best wine last."

Then Mary, the servants and the apostles realized that Jesus had turned the water to wine. This was the first miracle that Jesus performed.

(John 2:1–11)

THE SERMON ON THE MOUNT

Word of Jesus spread throughout the land, and wherever he went, large crowds gathered to hear him. He healed the sick and brought comfort to the poor and needy.

He preached to them of the kingdom of God, and how they could attain it. "Those who are sick or poor or hungry should rejoice, for they will receive their reward in heaven. But those who are rich and seek material gain on earth shall find no comfort there."

He preached compassion, humility and obedience to the commandments. Those who heard him were amazed by his words, for no one had ever spoken like him before.

(Matthew 5:7; Luke 6:17–49)

THE PARABLE OF THE PRODIGAL SON

Jesus often preached in parables so that his listeners could more easily understand. One day the lawyers were mocking him for welcoming the company of sinners. "One repentant sinner brings more rejoicing in heaven than ninety–nine good men who do not need forgiveness," Jesus told them.

"There was a man with two sons," he continued. "The younger asked for his share of money, then spent it recklessly. With none left, he decided to return to his father and beg forgiveness for his behavior. Humbly he went home and asked his father to treat him as a hired worker, for he was no longer worthy to be called his son. But his father called for a great feast to celebrate his son's return. The elder brother was angry because he had worked hard for his father but had never received such special treatment. The old man explained, 'My son, we must celebrate because your brother was lost to us, and now he is found.'"

(Luke 15:1–32)

THE WORKERS IN THE VINEYARD

Jesus explained to his followers that those who trust in earthly possessions will not reap rewards in heaven. Then he told a parable that shows that God gives His grace freely.

"A landowner hired men to work in his vineyards and promised them one coin," he told his listeners. "Towards the end of the day he saw men who still had no work and sent them to his vineyard too. When the work was finished, he paid his workers, beginning with those who had started last. He gave each of them one coin. Those who had worked since the beginning of the day expected more money since they had worked longer. When he gave them one coin also, they grumbled that they had done more work than the others. The landowner explained that no one gets less than he was promised. And all get more than they deserve."

(Matthew 19:23–30; 20:1–16)

92

THE GOOD SAMARITAN

One day while Jesus was preaching, a lawyer stood up and questioned him. "The law says that we should love our neighbor as ourselves," said the lawyer. "But who is my neighbor?"

In reply Jesus said, "A man was traveling to Jerusalem when robbers attacked him and left him for dead. Several people saw the man, but although they followed the law, they did nothing to help him. Instead they crossed to the other side of the road and passed him by.

"But then a Samaritan came by," said Jesus. "He helped the man, treated his wounds, and took him to an inn to recover. The next day he had to leave, but he gave the innkeeper money to look after the injured man."

Jesus turned to the lawyer. "Which of these men was a true neighbor?" he asked. And the lawyer replied, "The man who helped." "Go then and do likewise," said Jesus.

(Luke 10:25–37)

THE PARABLE OF THE SOWER

When a large crowd had gathered, Jesus said to them, "A farmer went out to sow his seed. As he scattered it, some fell on the path and was eaten by birds. Some fell among thorns and weeds and were choked. Some fell on rock, and produced plants that withered on the dry ground. Some seed fell on good soil, and the plants grew strong and plentiful."

When the disciples asked Jesus what the parable meant, he explained to them: "The seed that falls on the path is like those who hear the word of God but do not believe. The seed that falls on stony ground is like those who hear but do not maintain their faith. The seed choked by weeds represents people who get distracted by earthly worries.

"But the seed that falls on good soil stands for those who show their true conversion by keeping their faith and producing the fruit of obedience."

(Matthew 13:4–9; Luke 8:1–15)

JESUS HEALS THE SICK

One day some men brought their crippled friend to see Jesus. This man was paralyzed. His friends carried him on a mat. There was such a crowd around Jesus that the men climbed up onto the roof and lowered their friend into the room below.

When Jesus saw how strong their faith was, he healed the crippled man. "Friend, your sins are forgiven," he said. "Take your mat and go home."

Another time a Roman soldier approached Jesus as he was entering a town. He told Jesus that his faithful servant was dying. "I will come to him," said Jesus. But the soldier replied, "I do not ask you to go to my home, for I am not worthy. But only say the word and my servant shall be healed."

"Never have I seen such faith as yours," said Jesus. "Your servant shall live."

(Matthew 9:1–8; Luke 5:17–26; Matthew 8:5–13)

JESUS WALKS ON THE WATER

One day Jesus was teaching in a very remote place. As it grew dark, the apostles told Jesus that he should send the people away. "They will be hungry soon, and we have nothing for them here."

But Jesus took five loaves and two small fish and divided them among the apostles. "Pass this food around," he commanded. The apostles did not understand how this small amount of food could feed so many. But they did as Jesus asked. To their wonder, there was plenty of food for everyone.

After this miracle, Jesus went to pray by himself. The apostles took a boat to the other side of the lake, but a strong wind began to blow, and they became worried.

Suddenly they saw Jesus walking towards them across the water. They were terrified, but Jesus reassured them. "Come to me, Peter," he said. As soon as Peter stepped from the boat, he became afraid. "Help me, Lord!" he cried. "I will sink." Jesus helped Peter back on board. "What little faith you have," Jesus said. "Why did you doubt?"

(Matthew 14:13–31; Mark 8:1–9;
Luke 9:10–17; John 6:1–21)

THE TRANSFIGURATION

Jesus took three of his apostles, Peter, James and John, to the top of a high mountain. There Jesus was transfigured. His face shone as brilliantly as the sun, and his clothes became a blinding white. Moses and Elijah appeared beside him, bathed in the same light.

A bright cloud came down around them, and the apostles heard the voice of God. "This is My beloved Son. Listen to him."

In awe the three apostles fell to their knees. Jesus reached out to them, and told them not to be afraid. "You must go back now. But do not speak of what you have seen here until the Son of Man has risen again."

The apostles left Jesus, puzzled by his words.

(Matthew 17:1–9; Mark 9:2–13; Luke 9:28–36)

JESUS AND THE CHILDREN

Wherever Jesus went, parents brought their babies for him to touch and bless. Little children gathered around him as he preached, all trying to get as close to him as they could.

The apostles thought the children were bothering Jesus by crowding him. They tried to chase the children away, but Jesus stopped them. "Let the little children come to me. You know that the kingdom of God welcomes the weak and the small. You have heard me say this many times."

He pointed to the smallest child playing at his feet. "You should all be more like this child," he said to the listening crowd. "It is only with a child's trust and simplicity that you shall enter the Kingdom of God."

(Matthew 19:13–15; Mark 10:13–16; Luke 18:15–17)

LAZARUS

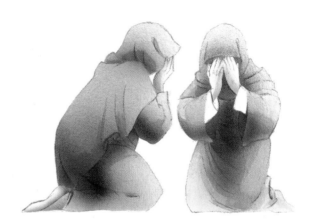

Lazarus, a friend of Jesus, was dying. His sisters, Mary and Martha, sent word to Jesus that Lazarus was ill. But when Jesus reached their home, Lazarus was already dead. Martha and Mary came to greet him. "Lord, if you had been with him when he was first ill," they sobbed, "he would have been healed." They took Jesus to the tomb where Lazarus had been laid to rest.

"Roll away the stone that covers the entrance," Jesus told them. Wondering, they did as he asked. Jesus looked up towards heaven. "Father, I know You have always heard my prayers. Now let everyone see that I do Your will."

Jesus faced the tomb and cried, "Lazarus, come out!" In joy and amazement the people watched as Lazarus walked out of the tomb.

(John 11:1–43)

JESUS ENTERS JERUSALEM

Although many people now believed in Jesus and the kingdom of God, he had powerful enemies. The high priests and lawyers saw him as a threat to their power. They tried to trap him with questions so they could arrest him. The people's love for Jesus frightened them.

When the feast of Passover came, no one believed Jesus would go to Jerusalem. The apostles begged him not to go. "You will surely be arrested," they cried. But they could not persuade him. Riding humbly on a donkey, Jesus entered the gates of Jerusalem.

Thousands had heard of his coming, and lined the road as he passed. They spread palm leaves on the road before him, and praised him as their Lord. "Blessed is he who comes in the name of the Lord!" they cried. "This is the prophet Jesus from Nazareth of Galilee."

(Matthew 21; Mark 11; 12:1–34; Luke 19:28–48; 20:1:39; John 7:25–44; 12:12–19)

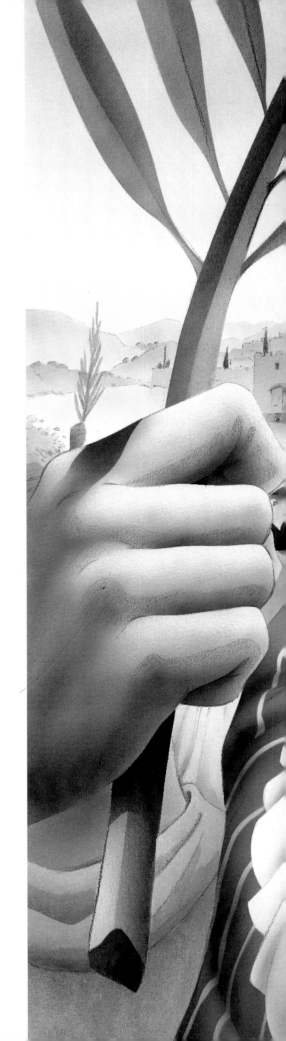

THE LAST SUPPER

Jesus knew that in Jerusalem he would be betrayed and put to death. He warned the apostles that this would be the last Passover feast he would ever share with them.

That evening Jesus and his apostles met in the room prepared for their meal. They were horrified when he told them, "This is the last night I will eat this bread and drink this wine. Some time tonight I will be arrested."

Then he took some bread, blessed it, broke it into pieces and divided it among the apostles. "This is my body," he told them. "I offer it as a sacrifice for all mankind. Eat it in memory of me."

Then he filled a cup with wine. "This is my blood," he said, passing it to each apostle in turn. "It will be shed for you and for all men. Drink this in memory of me."

(Matthew 16:21–28; 20:17–19; 26:17–30; Mark 8:31–38; 10:32–34; 14:12–26; Luke 18:31–34; 22:7–23; John 12:20–36; 13:18–21)

THE BETRAYAL

Jesus knew that one of his own disciples would betray him. Judas Iscariot had been tempted by Satan, and agreed to betray Jesus in return for thirty pieces of silver.

After the Last Supper, Jesus went to pray in the Garden of Gethsemene. A band of soldiers, led by Judas, arrived. "You should arrest the man I greet with a kiss," he told them. He went to Jesus and kissed him. "Have you betrayed me, Judas?" Jesus asked him sorrowfully. The other apostles wanted to fight so that Jesus could escape, but he went with the soldiers calmly.

Alone in the garden, Judas suddenly realized the terrible thing he had done. Crying out in horror, he threw the thirty pieces of silver to the ground in disgust. He could not live with the guilt of his betrayal and hanged himself.

(Matthew 26:14–16; 26:36–56; 27:1–10; Mark 14:32–50; Luke 22:1–6; 22:39–54, John 18:1–12)

JESUS BEFORE PILATE

Jesus was taken before the high council, known as the Sanhedrin. They questioned him harshly about his teachings and asked if he were the Son of God. "It is you who say so," replied Jesus. "But I will say this: One day you will see me sitting at the right hand of God and coming back on the clouds of heaven." With these words, Jesus acknowledged publicly that he was truly the Son of God.

The council accused Jesus of blasphemy, and took him to the Roman governor, Pontius Pilate. They demanded that Jesus be put to death, but Pilate could see no reason for such harshness.

It was the custom for the governor to release one prisoner during the Passover festival. The choice was between Jesus and a notorious criminal named Barabbas. Pilate asked whom he should release. "Release Barabbas!" cried the crowd." What shall I do with Jesus?" asked Pilate. "Let him be crucified!" shouted the crowd. Jesus was led away.

(Matthew 26:57–68; 27:11–26; Mark 14:53–65; 15:1–15;
Luke 22:66–71; 23:1–25; John 18:28–40; 19:1–16)

CARRYING THE CROSS

As the soldiers led Jesus out of the governor's palace, they mocked him cruelly. They beat him and spat at him, and placed a crown of thorns upon his head.

"Hail, King of the Jews!" they laughed.

The cross was brought forward, and Jesus was made to carry it on his shoulders through the streets. The soldiers forced a man called Simon, from Cyrene, to help Jesus bear the weight.

A large crowd followed Jesus, many of them weeping for him. "Do not weep for me," Jesus told them. "You should be weeping for yourselves and for your children, for there is much suffering ahead for you."

(Matthew 27:13–32; Mark 15:21–22; Luke 23:26–31; John 19:16–17)

116

THE CRUCIFIXION

The place of execution was called Golgotha, or Place of the Skull. Here the soldiers nailed Jesus to the cross and crucified him. Two robbers were crucified with him at the same time.

Above Jesus' head hung a sign that said, "The King of the Jews." The priests and lawyers came to mock Jesus. "He is the Son of God," they laughed. "And he cannot even save himself!"

After Jesus had hung on the cross for many hours, a heavy darkness spread across the land. Suddenly Jesus cried out, "My God, why have You forsaken me?" The crowd waited in awe to see what would happen.

Jesus cried out once more to God. Then his spirit left him, and he died. At the same moment the earth shook, and the temple curtain tore in two. The followers of Jesus took him down from the cross and laid him in a tomb.

(Matthew 27:32–56; Mark 15:21–41;
Luke 23:26–49; John 19:18–42)

THE RESURRECTION

After three days had passed, Mary Magdalene, one of the disciples, visited Jesus' tomb. To her dismay the tomb was open, and the body of Jesus was missing. As she began to weep, a shining angel appeared to her. "You should not be unhappy," said the angel. "You should be glad because Jesus has risen from the dead."

Then a voice called to her, and a man stood before her. At first she did not recognize him. Then to her great amazement and joy, her eyes were opened, and she saw that it was Jesus.

Full of awe and wonder, she hurried into town to tell the other disciples. Although Jesus had told them that the Son of God must die and rise again, they had not truly understood.

(Matthew 28:1–10; Mark 16:1–11; Luke 24:1–12; John 20:1–18)

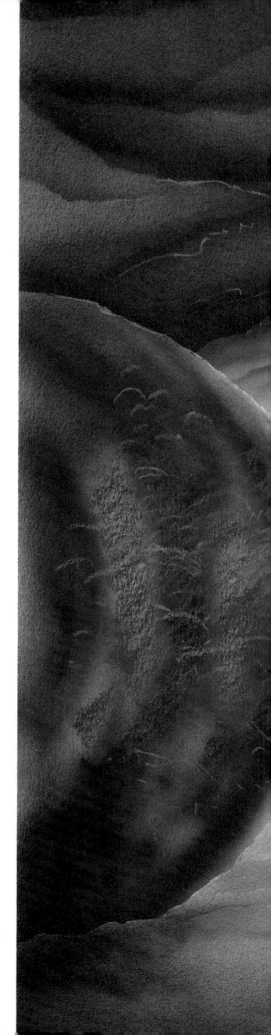

THE REVELATION

Later that day, Jesus appeared to two of his disciples as they traveled from Jerusalem to Emmaus. They did not recognize him, but welcomed him as a traveling companion. They spoke of Jesus of Nazareth and of his life and death. "Some claim to have seen Him risen from the tomb," one said, "but this is impossible." Jesus rebuked them explaining how the prophets had foretold that the Son of God would be crucified and rise from the dead.

The hour was late and they begged Jesus to stop with them for a meal. Jesus took bread, blessed it, broke it and gave it to them. They recognized him at once and, immediately, Jesus disappeared.

Later that evening a crowd including the apostles gathered. Suddenly Jesus appeared. They were afraid and thought he was a ghost. "Why do you doubt who I am? Touch me," Jesus said. "See the wounds in my hands and feet. I am no ghost."

(Mark 16:12–14; Luke 24:13–48; John 19:30)

THE ASCENSION

The apostles went out to the Mount of Olives, were they had once prayed with Jesus. There he appeared to them for the last time. "You must prepare," he told them. "The Holy Spirit will soon come upon you. On that day you must go out and spread the word of God to all nations. You must teach mankind all that you have seen and learned while I was with you."

Jesus then blessed the apostles, who bowed their heads in worship. He had finished talking with them. At that moment he was taken into heaven, and sits at God's right hand.

And just as Jesus had said, the Holy Spirit came upon the apostles and gave them the strength and wisdom to go out and preach the word of God.

Wherever they traveled many people listened, many believed. And many turned to God, just as Jesus had foretold.

(Matthew 28:16–20; Mark 16:15–20; Luke 24:44–53; John 20:21)

124